Lots of things
you want to know about
PIRATES

...and some
you don't!

Written and Illustrated
by David West

Smart Apple Media

Published by Smart Apple Media, an imprint of Black Rabbit Books
P.O. Box 3263, Mankato, Minnesota 56002
www.smartapplemedia.com

Produced by David West ♟ Children's Books
6 Princeton Court, 55 Felsham Road, London SW15 1AZ

Designed and illustrated by David West

Copyright © 2013 David West Children's Books

Library of Congress Cataloging-in-Publication Data

West, David, 1956-
Lots of things you want to know about pirates... and some you don't! / David West.
pages cm. – (Lots of things you want to know about)
Includes index.
ISBN 978-1-62588-092-5
1. Pirates–Juvenile literature. I. Title.
G535.W47 2014
910.4'5–dc23
5-31-16   2013030756
Printed in China
CPSIA compliance information DWCB15CP
311214

9 8 7 6 5 4 3 2 1

Contents

Buccaneers and Corsairs Were Other Names for Pirates

Buccaneers were pirates from the Caribbean Sea. Their name comes from the word "buccan," a wooden frame they used to smoke fish and meat on the island of Hispaniola.

Corsairs like the Barbary corsairs from North Africa raided ships and ports in the Mediterranean Sea and North Atlantic Ocean. They had fast ships that used oars as well as sails.

A Pirate's Flag Was Called a "Jolly Roger"

The Jolly Roger flag had a skull and crossbones on a black background. It was flown to frighten pirates' victims into surrendering without a fight.

Many pirates developed their own Jolly Rogers. Calico Jack Rackham had crossed swords instead of bones. Blackbeard flew the devil spearing a red heart.

Pirates' Ships Were Small and Fast

Pirates used small ships called sloops and caravels. They were fast and could turn quickly. This meant they could catch slower trading ships filled with riches.

These small ships had a shallower **draft**, which allowed them to dart up shallow rivers and creeks to escape larger navy warships that were sent to catch them.

Some Pirate Victims Walked the Plank

Some pirates would make their **captives** walk the plank to scare them into telling them where their gold was hidden. If the victims ended up in the water, they could drown or be eaten by sharks. Walking the plank was rare, though. Usually victims were simply thrown overboard if the pirates did not like them.

Pirates Had Rules

Most pirates had a set of rules called the code of **conduct**. They voted who would be captain and could vote him out again at any time. There were no officers, as pirates hated people telling them what to do.

One rule said that there was no fighting on board the ship. Quarrels had to be resolved on land with a pistol or sword. The **quartermaster** would make sure that it was a fair fight. A fight to the death was rare. Usually a fight ended when a pirate drew blood.

Pirates Shared Their Treasure Equally

The pirate code stated that any **loot** plundered had to be shared equally. The quartermaster figured out who got what. This could be quite difficult when the loot was made up of silks and jewels.

Gold coins were often cut up to make sure everyone got their fair share.

Some Pirates Were Marooned on Desert Islands

If a pirate was found guilty of breaking the rules, he could be punished by being marooned. Generally a marooned man was left on a deserted island, often no more than a sand bar at low tide. He would be given some food, a container of water, and a loaded pistol.

Marooning often ended in death, but some men survived. Captain Edward England was marooned with two crew members on the island of Mauritius in the Indian Ocean. They built a small raft and made it safely to a port in Madagascar.

Pirates Kept Pets

Pets such as parrots and monkeys were popular among all sailors. Pirates in the Caribbean traded cloth and other goods for these **exotic** animals.

Exotic pets were popular because they fetched high prices in Europe. This was especially true of the colorful parrots and macaws that could be taught to say words.

Pirates Liked to Sing

The most valuable members of the crew were carpenters, **navigators**, and musicians. Pirates loved a good song and a dance. They even sang when they hauled up the sails.

One pirate code of conduct was that musicians rested on Sundays. This was a good thing, because at any time a crew member could ask a musician to strike up a tune.

Some Pirates Went to Bed at 8 O'clock

The pirate's day was long and hard. When the sun went down, there was little to do except catch up on some sleep. The pirate captain Bartholomew Roberts's code of conduct number 4 said:

"The lights and candles should be put out at eight at night, and if any of the crew desire to drink after that hour they shall sit upon the open deck without lights."

Pirates Had Injury Insurance

Life as a pirate was full of danger. Many pirates lost a limb from cannon fire but survived to tell the tale. Pirates donated a certain amount of their ill-gotten gains to help those who had been injured.

One pirate code of conduct stated, "Every man who shall become a cripple or lose a limb in the service shall have 800 pieces of eight from the common stock."

Some Pirates Had Peg Legs

The famous French pirate captain François Le Clerc was wounded fighting the English in 1549. He replaced his amputated leg with a wooden one. Despite his disability Le Clerc led successful raids against the Spanish, who nicknamed him "Peg Leg."

He died in 1563 while attacking Spanish treasure ships.

Black Bart Liked to Drink Tea

Pirates liked to drink lots of rum. In fact, they liked to drink any type of **liquor**. The famous pirate captain Bartholomew Roberts, known as Black Bart, was different.

Black Bart had a fearsome reputation and was one of the most successful pirates of all time. Although he might occasionally drink a mug of ale, his preferred drink was a nice cup of tea!

17

Pirates Buried Their Treasure

Pirate **booty** was usually food, drink, and clothing. When they did get gold, they would spend it, although there are a few stories of pirates burying their treasure.

Captain Kidd buried treasure on Gardiner's Island, near Long Island, New York. Most of it was recovered when he was arrested, but people still hunt for the rest of it today.

Blackbeard's Real Name Was Edward Teach

Blackbeard was a well-known English pirate. He attacked ships around the West Indies and the eastern coast of America from 1716 to 1718.

His nickname came from his large black beard in which he twisted lengths of lighted fuse. He did this to scare his enemies when he attacked their ships.

Blackbeard's short career came to an end in 1718 when he died after attacking British naval ships sent to capture him.

Not All Pirates Were Men

Some famous pirates were women, such as Anne Bonny and Mary Read. They were members of John "Calico Jack" Rackham's crew.

They both wore men's clothing and were ferocious fighters. They were captured in 1780, along with Rackham, and were sent to a prison in Jamaica. Mary died in prison but Anne escaped and disappeared forever.

Mary Read Beat a Pirate in a Sword Fight

When Mary Read discovered her pirate boyfriend had to fight a duel with another pirate, she knew he would lose. She insulted the other pirate so that he would have to fight her first.

When her boyfriend turned up to fight, he found the pirate dead. Mary had killed him in a sword fight.

Mrs. Cheng Owned the Biggest Pirate Fleet

Cheng I Sao and her husband led a large group of pirates that eventually numbered more than 50,000. When her husband died in 1807, Mrs. Cheng assumed command.

Their fleet consisted of 200 ocean-going **junks**, 600–800 coastal boats, and dozens of small river boats.

Glossary

booty another word for treasure

captives people who have been captured

conduct behavior

draft the distance between the water level and the bottom of a ship

exotic from foreign lands

insurance a contract in which a group of people pay out money to others for a loss that is stated in the contract

junk ancient Chinese sailing vessels; their design is still used today

liquor a strong alcoholic drink

loot another word for treasure

navigators important members of a ship's crew who use charts and experience to get a ship safely from one place to another

quartermaster the second most important crew member after the captain

Index